Edvard Grieg

by Wendy Thompson

OTHER TITLES IN THE SERIES
Johann Sebastian Bach by Charlotte Gray (1-85015-311-6)
Ludwig van Beethoven by Pam Brown (1-85015-302-7)
Leonard Bernstein by David Wilkins (1-85015-595-X)
Frédéric Chopin by Pam Brown (1-85015-310-8)
Claude Debussy by Roderic Dunnett (1-85015-397-6)
Antonin Dvŏrák by Roderic Dunnett (1-85015-596-8)
Elton John by John O'Mahony (1-85015-369-8)
John Lennon by Michael White (1-85015-304-3)
Bob Marley by Marsha Bronson (1-85015-312-4)
Wolfgang Amadeus Mozart by Michael White (1-85015-300-0)
Franz Schubert by Barrie Carson-Turner (1-85015-598-4)
Peter Ilych Tchaikovsky by Michael Pollard (1-85015-303-5)
Antonio Vivaldi by Pam Brown (1-85015-301-9)

Picture credits: AKG London: 13, 16, 31 (top), 54, 58, 60 (right); Ann Ronan: 4, 9 (both), 12 (bottom left and right), 24, 29, 41, 55; Art Studio/Egil Korsnes: 8 (both), 11, 17, 18, 20, 25 (bottom), 26, 28, 31 (bottom), 38, 40, 42 (left), 45, 49, 57, 59; Bridgeman Art Library: 12 (left), 14-15, 22 (left), 22-23, 27, 44/Giraudon, 48; Hulton Deutsch Collection Limited: 25 (top)/Erich Auerbach; Image Select: 5, 7, 10, 14, 23 (right), 30, 42 (right), 52, 53, 55, 60 (left); Mary Evans Picture Library: 6; Bergen Public Library: 21, 33 (top), 34-35; National Museum Stockholm: 33 (bottom); Ole A Buenget/Samfoto: 19, 50-51; Performing Arts Library/Clive Barda 36-37: ZEFA/TEASY: 39.

The Publishers would like to extend a special thanks to the Grieg Museum, Bergen and Bergen Public Library for their help on picture research.

Published in Great Britain in 1995
by Exley Publications Ltd,
16 Chalk Hill, Watford,
Herts WD1 4BN, United Kingdom.

A copy of the CIP data is available from the British Library on request.

ISBN 1-85015-488-0

Series editor: Samantha Armstrong
Editorial assistants: Helen Lanz and
Alison MacTier
Musical adviser: Jill Simms
Picture editors: Alex Goldberg and James Clift
of Image Select
Typeset by Delta Print, Watford, Herts, U.K.
Printed at Oriental Press, U.A.E.

Edvard
GRIEG

by Wendy Thompson

≣EXLEY

*Opposite: Edvard Grieg
aged about thirty. He
was described as having
characteristics typical
of his home town,
"[a] lively Bergen
fellow, outspoken,
quick-tempered,
and enthusiastic."*

Norway's great composer

It is a Sunday morning in Hardanger, Norway in 1877. In the village schoolroom by the fjord, deserted by the children for the summer, sits Norway's most famous composer, Edvard Grieg. He is watching people rowing past on their way to church. He sighs and bends back over his music manuscript, writing first in pencil, erasing and correcting many times until satisfied, and then inking over the pencil.

Suddenly Grieg is distracted by the shouts of children. They come tumbling round the hut, peering through the windows, yelling and jostling. They are some of the large family of his landlords, Hans and Brita Utne, dressed in their Sunday best – the bright embroidered costumes of Hardanger peasant folk. Edvard Grieg sighs again. The schoolroom is too close to the village for the peace and quiet he needs to compose.

*Below: Composers often
need peace and quiet
for their work although
Johann Sebastian Bach
managed to write his
music in a noisy,
cramped apartment full
of children next to a
schoolroom. Edvard
Grieg hated to be
watched while he was
composing, however,
and persuaded fifty
local villagers to
transport his log cabin
up the mountain to a
more secluded spot.*

Composing

The next day Grieg abandons the schoolroom and moves to a log hut on the water's edge, with a breathtaking view of the Folgefonn Glacier, high in the mountains across the fjord. The hut is tiny, just big enough for a piano, a table, and a chair. Grieg settles down to work, trying out his ideas on the piano. But again he is interrupted – this time by hushed voices outside. He goes out to find himself confronting a small, huddled crowd of curious onlookers, who have come to find out what is going on at the "tune-house."

The Battle of Culloden, Scotland, fought on April 16, 1746. Bonnie Prince Charlie tried to rally enough people to unseat England's King George II, but was defeated by English forces at Culloden. Some thirty years later Edvard Grieg's great grandfather left Scotland to make a better life for himself in Norway.

The following day about fifty burly, local men march down to the log hut, and, grunting with strain, haul the entire structure further up the mountain on wooden rollers, to a more secluded spot that Edvard Grieg has found. The whole process takes nearly a day.

In the evening, food and drink flow freely. Grieg celebrates by playing some of his folk dances on the piano to the villagers, who begin to join in. Jogging and bobbing to the vigorous rhythms of their local dances, the villagers suddenly leap into the air in a frenzy, as though they have wings. Grieg listens, his head nodding in time to the music, offering glasses of wine to the hot and sweaty dancers. This is the Norway he loves.

In the beginning

Edvard Grieg – whose Piano Concerto and music for Henrik Ibsen's play, *Peer Gynt* are played all over the world – is firmly associated with the music and scenery of Norway and its mountains, fjords, and rough, peasant dances. His story, however, begins across the North Sea, in Scotland, where his ancestor, Alexander Greig, was born in 1739.

When Alexander was seven years old, the Scottish Jacobites, led by Bonnie Prince Charlie, were

defeated by the English on the bloody battlefield of Culloden. Bitter years of humiliation and economic hardship for the Scots followed, and against this background, Alexander Greig decided to make the break and emigrated to Norway.

Bergen, the busy, noisy little Norwegian port where Alexander chose to settle, had already proved a haven for many independent Scottish people. It was sheltered from the icy east wind by mountain ranges and thronged with fishermen shouting in gruff, guttural voices as they traded on the quayside. Here, Alexander did rather well for himself. Before long he had built up a thriving fishing and lobster fleet. He married, took Norwegian citizenship, and changed his name to the Norwegian spelling, "Grieg."

A drawing of the Bergen waterfront, done in 1870, when Edvard Grieg would have known it. In the seaport town of Bergen, fishing was of major importance for families like the Griegs, both as a source of income and as a way of life.

The Grieg family

Alexander's grandson, Alexander, who became Edvard's father, carried on the family fishing business and continued to rise in society. He became a solid, prosperous, middle-class citizen who took an active interest not only in the town's trade, but also in its cultural life.

The town of Bergen was founded in late medieval times by merchants from the southern shores of the Baltic, and just like its German counterparts such as the city port of Hamburg, culture flourished alongside business. Edvard Grieg later paid tribute to the town of his birth, "My material has been drawn from the surroundings of Bergen. Its natural beauty, the life of its people, the city's achievements and all sorts of activities have been an inspiration to me. I find the smell of the German Quay exciting; in fact, I'm sure my music tastes of codfish."

Musical background

In the eighteenth and nineteenth centuries Bergen was home to poets, painters, musicians, and playwrights. Its lively musical society provided stimulation and entertainment for the people – and especially the women – of Bergen.

Above: Edvard Grieg's father and mother, Alexander and Gesine. Grieg enjoyed a good relationship with both his parents; with his mother who encouraged his musical talents and his father with whom he shared an active correspondence throughout his life. Below: The first photograph of Edvard Grieg, aged nine.

Alexander married Gesine Judith Hagerup, who wrote poems and plays and was also a fine amateur pianist. Middle-class women in the nineteenth century did not usually work outside the home, but developed their musical skills – especially piano playing and singing – for recreation and for the instruction of their children. Alexander and Gesine had five children. The fourth child, Edvard, born on June 15, 1843, inherited his mother's musical and poetic talents.

Childhood

Edvard was brought up in a town house on one of Bergen's oldest streets, just off a maze of narrow alleyways swarming with tumbledown houses. The Grieg household was a model of middle-class respectability. As a child, Edvard listened to his mother playing piano pieces by Mozart, Beethoven, and Chopin, and when he was six, he had his first piano lesson with her.

He was a quick learner but hated scales and exercises. Instead, he preferred to improvise, exploring different harmonies. When he was nine,

his family moved three miles (5km) outside Bergen, and Edvard and his older brother John had to walk to school every day. Edvard hated school and later spoke about some of his methods for playing truant whenever he could. The teachers were rude and sarcastic about his early efforts at composing music, and he found the atmosphere cold, harsh, and

It was Edvard's mother, especially, who realized that there was something unusual about Edvard's talent, for his musical imagination and joy in creating were evident in the fact that he liked nothing better than to sit and daydream at the piano."

F. Benestad and
Dag Schjelderup-Ebbe, from Edvard
Grieg The Man and the Artist.

PÅ DETTE STED LÅ
BARNDOMSHJEMMET TIL

EDVARD GRIEG

1843-1907

HUSET BLE ØDELAGT I
EKSPLOSJONSULYKKEN PÅ VÅGEN
20. APRIL 1944

A house in Bergen on the street where Edvard Grieg was born. The plaque commemorates the birthplace of Norway's most famous composer.

unsympathetic. He endured this torment for five more miserable years, but one day, when he was still only fifteen, his life changed dramatically.

Ole Bull

Into the courtyard of the Griegs' home, mounted on a handsome thoroughbred Arabian horse, rode a flamboyant figure, a national hero, Ole Bull.

Ole Bull was not only one of the most brilliant violinists of his time, but through his close identification with Norwegian culture, he played a leading role in Norway's struggle to free itself from centuries of foreign domination. Norway had, for four hundred years, been ruled by Denmark.

Ole Bull, famous Norwegian violinist, romantic adventurer, and nationalist who encouraged Norwegian writers and artists in their work and had a significant effect on the career of Grieg.

Born in Bergen in 1810, Ole Bull had begun to play in the town's orchestra at the age of only nine, before beginning an international career which took him all over Europe. When he was twenty-five, he appeared at a gala concert at the Paris Opera, describing himself as a "Norwegian artist." Wherever he played, Ole Bull included his own pieces and improvisations based on the lively rhythms and melodies of Norwegian folk dances.

He also loved the national instruments such as the Hardanger fiddle and he tried to copy its unique sound in his own virtuoso violin playing. Soon influential critics started to talk and write enthusiastically about Norway and its flourishing art. Ole Bull had made his point successfully.

On his return to Norway from a trip to the United States in 1848, Ole Bull announced his intention of preserving and promoting Norwegian art by setting up a National Theater in Bergen. It would present plays by Norwegian playwrights in Norwegian.

All through history, powerful countries have dominated and ruled over smaller countries by suppressing their languages – the symbol of a country's national identity. The Norwegian language had for many centuries been regarded as second class and had been suppressed. Danish was regarded as the only language suitable for cultured people.

"It was Ole Bull who first awakened in me the resolution to compose characteristically Norwegian music.... Through him I became acquainted with many forgotten folk songs, and above all with my own nature."

Edvard Grieg, from Talks with Great Composers, by Arthur Abel.

Musical direction

On meeting Ole Bull, fifteen year old Edvard Grieg remembered, "I felt something like an electric current pass right through me when his hand touched mine." Ole Bull listened intently as Edvard played a few of his own pieces on the piano, and then told his astonished parents that Edvard should go to Leipzig, to study at the Conservatory. So a few

The Leipzig Conservatory which was located in cramped quarters in the Gewandhaus during the time when Edvard Grieg was a student there. Later, in 1887, it moved to the more spacious premises in the Grassistrasse.

11

months later, in October 1858, Edvard Grieg set sail for Germany "like a parcel stuffed with dreams."

Grieg may have hated school, but he hated the Leipzig Conservatory more. Leipzig, one of Germany's major cities for trade and cultural life, had a long tradition of musical education. J. S. Bach had taught at the Thomasschule for over twenty-five years, while talented students from the university had fed the city's many choral societies and orchestras. The Conservatory itself was founded in 1843 by the composer Mendelssohn, who was its first director. Schumann had also taught there. Although it had

Below: Robert Schumann, to whose music Grieg was particularly drawn. Through it he found expression of his own Romantic spirit.

Above: Johann Sebastian Bach whom Grieg regarded as one of the greatest musicians of all time. He once said, "I make no pretensions of being in the class with Bach, [his] works are eternal...."

only been in existence for fifteen years, it had already built up a reputation as one of Europe's leading teaching institutions – a place where aspiring young musicians begged to be sent.

But when Grieg arrived, he was utterly miserable. Stuck in the middle of the flat, central German plain, he missed the clean, fresh air of the Norwegian mountains and sea. He felt stifled by the routine, the discipline, the endless rules and regulations of academic life. His piano teacher, Louis Plaidy, was a stern disciplinarian who insisted on his students working through dry studies and exercises, which Grieg loathed.

Schumann's influence

After a few months, Grieg was so unhappy that he asked to be transferred to another teacher. He was placed with a close friend of the late Robert Schumann's, Wenzel, who introduced him to the glories of Schumann's music. He was later taught by Moscheles, a great pianist through whom Grieg learned to appreciate the piano sonatas of Beethoven. Although he later claimed that he "learned nothing at the Conservatory," his sketchbooks show that his composition teachers encouraged his early efforts.

Another positive aspect of student life at Leipzig was the wealth of music-making all around, especially the orchestral concerts given by the famous Leipzig Gewandhaus Orchestra. At one of these concerts Grieg heard Clara Schumann, the

Opposite right: Felix Mendelssohn, founder of the Leipzig Conservatory and conductor of the Leipzig Gewandhaus Orchestra from 1835.

Clara Schumann, wife of Robert, who combined the heavy demands of family life with a brilliant international career as a concert pianist. Grieg loved to hear her play and would attend her European concert tours whenever he could.

Edvard Grieg holding his graduation certificate from the Leipzig Conservatory. About his time as a student there, he later claimed, "I was awkward, sluggish, unattractive, and quite unteachable."

brilliant concert pianist whose husband Robert had recently died, play Schumann's Piano Concerto – a work which was to influence his own famous concerto many years later.

Illness strikes

In the spring of 1860, when Edvard Grieg was seventeen, he was stricken with a dangerous lung infection which severely damaged his health. He was rushed home to his mother's care in Bergen to spend the summer recovering. After the summer he was well enough to return to Leipzig, where he stayed for another eighteen months.

At his graduation concert in April 1862, Grieg played three of his *Four Piano Pieces,* and he accompanied his *Four Songs for Alto* on the piano. He left the Leipzig Conservatory with glowing reports from his teachers – "an outstanding pianist," "one of the best of our composition students" – but he was under-confident about his own abilities.

"He played everything with the utmost delicacy and an unusually attractive, supple, fine-sounding touch which I have never heard before. In so doing he brought out the unique characteristics of each piece – something that only the composer can accomplish."

A critic from Musical Courier, New York, January, 1897.

Many years later, he recalled his student years, saying "It was fortunate for me that in Leipzig I was able to hear so much fine music, especially orchestral and chamber music. This compensated for the training in composition that I failed to get...." He also commented, "I didn't accomplish anything during those three years that would create any expectation for the future."

> **"I was anything but an outstanding conservatory student. Quite the opposite. At the beginning I was lazy to the core."**
>
> *Edvard Grieg,*
> *from his article,*
> *"My First Success."*

First fruits

On returning to Bergen after graduating from Leipzig, Edvard Grieg found himself out of work and with little scope for finding any. Ole Bull's National Theater in Bergen had had to shut down temporarily due to lack of funds, and the Harmonic Society only offered scope for amateur music-making.

Grieg's thoughts for his future turned to the Danish capital Copenhagen, then the major city for cultural life in all of Scandinavia. Copenhagen was

The vegetable market in Copenhagen, the city where Edvard Grieg sought work after graduating. It was a place of European culture, which could offer work to artists, writers, and musicians.

15

the place where Norwegian, Swedish, and Finnish intellectuals were most likely to find suitable jobs.

So in the spring of 1863, Grieg now went to Copenhagen, where he was to spend the next three years. Here he made contact with the Danish composer Niels Gade, who was to play an important role in Grieg's own development as a composer.

Shortly after arriving in Copenhagen, Edvard Grieg timidly ventured to visit Niels Gade, taking with him the piano pieces and songs he had performed at his graduation concert. Gade was not interested in such small pieces. He brusquely waved them aside and told Grieg to get on with a major piece, such as a symphony. Grieg soon found that this was a tall order as he was more talented at composing smaller scale works, but he struggled on and completed a Symphony in C minor by May 2, 1864. He was twenty. It was first heard a month

Niels Gade, the Danish composer who had an important influence over Grieg in his early years. Grieg came to value Gade's advice and knowledge, claiming that it was because of him that he returned to Denmark.

later, and twice in Bergen in 1867, but by then Grieg was embarrassed by it, and decided it was never to be performed again.

Romance

In Copenhagen, Edvard Grieg also made contact with one of his cousins, Nina Hagerup, who, at eighteen, was just two years younger than him.

Although Nina was born in Bergen, she had spent most of her life in Denmark. Tiny, like Edvard, and very pretty, Nina had a beautiful singing voice and an instinctive feel for poetry. "She sang as a bird sings, as though the idea of which she was singing were being born at that instant," a relative recalled many years later. "She laid bare the innermost feelings of her soul.... Her voice was like an inexhaustible well." A journalist of the time wrote, "... as far as I know everyone who has had the pleasure of hearing her has felt the same.... As soon

Edvard Grieg and his wife, Nina Hagerup. They were married for forty years and their marriage was, basically, a happy one, although marred by the death of their only child, and by Grieg's reputed affairs with other women.

Rikard Nordraak in Copenhagen, 1865. Nordraak awakened Grieg's interest in Norwegian folk culture, especially its customs, its literature, and its music. He was one of the earliest Norwegian composers who tried to translate the sounds and sights of the country into music. "When grief and worry threatened," he wrote, "water-sprite played and the fairy-folk danced to me so that I forgot everything but the sounds from over in Norway.... And what I heard, I wrote down."

as [she] has begun to sing one forgets that one is in a concert hall. We suffer with her, we weep, laugh and rejoice with her from the beginning to the end."

Edvard was instantly smitten, and in July 1864, a month after the first performance of his symphony, he and Nina became engaged. From then on, he began to write songs for Nina, including four "Romances" – as the Danish referred to the lyric songs Grieg preferred to work with – and *Melodies of the Heart*, settings of Danish lyrics by Hans Christian Andersen, famous for his fairy stories, such as *The Snow Queen* and *The Little Tin Soldier.*

Many years later, Grieg wrote to an American biographer, "How does it happen that my songs play such an important part in my life? Quite simply owing to the circumstances that even I, like other mortals, was for once in my life endowed with genius (to quote Goethe). The flash of genius was – love. I loved a young girl who had a wonderful voice and an equally wonderful gift of interpretation. That girl became my wife and my lifelong companion to this very day. For me she has been – I dare admit it – the only genuine interpreter of my songs."

Friendship

During his years in Copenhagen, Grieg met someone else who was to have a profound influence on the rest of his own life. Born of a Danish mother and Norwegian father, twenty-two year old Rikard Nordraak mesmerized everyone who came into contact with him. He was not especially witty or amusing, but he was passionately interested in people and ideas, especially anything to do with Norway – its culture and its history.

Nordraak loved the country and its people, especially its native folk culture – its dances and songs, its old tales and its festivals. A talented pianist,

Nordraak also dabbled in composition, inspired, he said, by the legends of Norway – its mythical water-sprites and fairy-folk. His pieces were not technically brilliant, but they were striking and unusual. Many were influenced by the characteristic sounds of Norwegian folk music, especially the sound of the folk instrument called the Hardanger fiddle.

Norwegian folk instruments

The Hardanger fiddle – as loved by Ole Bull – looks like a small, narrow violin, with a highly arched body, a short neck, a low bridge, and a flat fingerboard, which is often beautifully decorated with ivory or mother-of-pearl. It has four strings, like an ordinary violin, but beneath those is another set of four or five, called "sympathetic strings," since when the upper strings are bowed, the lower ones vibrate in sympathy, making an ethereal, silvery sound. Because the bridge is so flat, the player can play on more than one string at the same time (which is quite difficult on a normal violin), giving the characteristic rough sound of chords (two or more notes played simultaneously), or of a drone (one string which sounds all the time, like a drone of a bagpipe).

A procession of Norwegian peasants, led by a traditional folk fiddler. Grieg's contact with the folk culture of Norway influenced all of his music, and he became friendly with several of Norway's leading folk fiddlers.

In Grieg's time, the Hardanger fiddle was usually held low down against the player's chest, but modern instruments are now played under the chin, more like a normal violin. Norwegians used the Hardanger fiddle to accompany a wide range of folk dances (*slåtter* in Norwegian), including the *halling*. This was one of the most traditional dances from Grieg's own Bergen district, in which the dancers start in a relaxed, heavy manner, almost as if they are in a dream, and then get livelier and faster, until suddenly they sink down again, and the dance ends as it began.

A variety of sounds

The Hardanger fiddle was just one of the folk instruments that Norwegian composers used; another was the *langeleik*, a type of zither that dated back to medieval times. It had two melody strings played by a plectrum, and the other drone strings were played by the fingers.

While it was usually men who played the Hardanger fiddle, the *langeleik* was also a women's instrument, played indoors to accompany folk songs. Another sound that Grieg and Nordraak would have heard from their childhood would have been the *lokk*, special vocal techniques which sounded like a deep-throated, highly ornamental yodel, used by peasant women to call their cows from the high mountain pastures. One of the pieces in Grieg's *Twenty-five Norwegian Dances and Songs* for piano is based on this unique sound.

Grieg and folk music

All these typical Norwegian sounds had found their way into Nordraak's music, and now also began to influence the young Grieg's.

Throughout his life, Edvard Grieg made many transcriptions and arrangements – mostly for piano – of genuine Norwegian folk melodies, which he heard when he went walking in the remote mountain regions. But all his music was influenced by the characteristic techniques of Norwegian folk music, especially its jagged, dotted rhythms, its harmonies

Below: A Norwegian Hardanger fiddler. The player holds the fiddle against his chest, not under his chin, like an ordinary violin, and the instrument is beautifully decorated with inlaid woods. The Hardanger fiddle was used to accompany a wide range of folk dances.

Opposite: The Funeral March of Rikard Nordraak, written by Edvard Grieg. The memory and influence of Nordraak stayed with the composer all of his life. On his last concert tours he actually carried a copy of this music in case he died abroad.

in imitation of drone basses, and its highly ornamented melodies which tend to repeat themselves in short phrases. Grieg's Piano Concerto has a clear Norwegian influence from its very opening and is based on the three-note melodic formula that Grieg liked so much and that goes all the way down the keyboard.

Grieg and Nordraak

Brought together by their passionate interest in folk music, Grieg and Nordraak became close friends. In 1865, Grieg went to visit the sights of Zealand (in north Denmark) with his friends Feddersen and Horneman. Nordraak had hoped to spend the winter with Grieg in Italy, in search of sun, wine, and cheap living. But while Grieg still lingered among the beech-woods and heather-covered moors of Zealand, Nordraak went on ahead to Berlin.

In October, Grieg joined him there, but shortly

Above: The Old Museum in Berlin, a city that Grieg visited in October 1865, and where his friend Nordraak became unwell and died of tuberculosis. Right: A view of the Bay of Naples in the nineteenth century. If they could afford it, young men such as Grieg visited as much of Europe as possible to improve their cultural education. Grieg recognized the importance of broadening his outlook, writing of, "...an openness of mind, such as can only be gained when one's eyes are opened to what can be learnt in the South. There a freer and more universal view of the world and art begins to unfold."

after his arrival, Nordraak contracted tuberculosis – a disease which, until the discovery of antibiotics in the mid-twentieth century, was the major killer of young and old alike. Apparently unaware of the seriousness of Nordraak's illness – or perhaps because he feared he might catch it himself – Grieg hurriedly went on to Rome, leaving his friend alone in Berlin. He ignored Nordraak's anguished letters begging him to return to his friend's bedside and, six months later, while Grieg enjoyed himself among the ancient wonders of Rome, Naples, and Pompeii, the young man died.

Stricken with remorse, Grieg, now twenty-two, wrote a funeral march in his friend's memory and visited his grave in Berlin on the way home to Norway. To Nordraak's father he wrote, "It shall be the task of my life to carry on the work in his spirit. I feel the responsibility.... We had hoped to work together for the advancement of our national art; since that has been denied us, all I can do is hold

Above: The Colosseum in Rome, which Grieg visited in April 1866, aged twenty-two. He was scandalized to hear the operatic music of Bellini, Rossini, and Donizetti which he found "Terrible music" being sung in Italian churches.

faithfully to the promise I gave him that his cause should be my cause, his goal mine. Do not believe that his aspirations will be forgotten...."

Move to Christiania

On his return from Italy, Grieg decided that the best way to carry out his mission was to move to the capital of Norway, Christiania (renamed Oslo in 1924). There, on October 15, 1866, he introduced himself to the public in a concert of his own works, including a violin sonata and a piano sonata, all written the previous year. Nina sang songs by Grieg and his friends, including Nordraak. The concert was a great success, and soon after, Grieg was invited to become conductor of the amateur Christiania Philharmonic Society.

From then on, conducting was to be an important part of Grieg's life. Up to the time of Beethoven, orchestras had usually been directed from the keyboard and often by the composer himself. Later in the nineteenth century, however, the keyboard instrument disappeared from orchestras, which

Richard Wagner, a German opera composer, whose music was studied by all the students of the Leipzig Conservatory. Grieg disliked Wagner's vocal music and style of composition, but couldn't help admiring his genius, describing one of his musical dramas as, "...the work of a giant."

became bigger as music became more complex. The only way to keep the players together was to have a conductor standing at the front keeping time with a small stick, or baton. The principles of modern conducting were laid down by Wagner and Berlioz, who both understood the complicated role that a conductor must play in interpreting the composer's intentions, and communicating them to the orchestra, as well as just keeping time.

Grieg the conductor

Grieg was a sensitive conductor. Claude Debussy – no admirer of Grieg's music – paid tribute to his conducting skills when he saw him in Paris at the age of fifty-nine, "Despite his age, he is lively and sparing, and conducts the orchestra with a disquieting attention to detail, underlining all the nuances and nurturing feeling for the music with tireless care."

In the 1860s, conductors were not treated with the respect they command today. Although Christiania was the capital of Norway, it was still a cultural backwater and Grieg found it difficult to interest the local population in music. However, he went ahead with his concerts, bringing works such as Mendelssohn's *Elijah*, Mozart's *Requiem,* and some pieces by Scandinavian composers to public attention. In the end, his persistence in the teeth of

Above: A modern conductor, using his baton to control and direct the orchestra. Grieg was as highly respected for his conducting as he was for his music.

Below: One of Grieg's concerts in Christiania. He introduced works such as Mozart's Requiem *to Norwegian audiences.*

what he saw as indifference and philistinism paid off. After four years, he persuaded the Musical Society to take on some professional orchestral players, and this orchestra ultimately developed into the Oslo Philharmonic, which has since become an orchestra of international standing.

From *Lyric Pieces* to the Piano Concerto

In 1867 Edvard and Nina married and settled in a small apartment in Christiania. Their first year together was very happy and, during that time, Grieg began to write some little piano pieces, which he collected together under the title *Lyric Pieces*. These charming, unpretentious miniatures, seeped in the rhythms and melodies of Norwegian folk music, are now among his best-known works – all young people learning the piano will learn at least some of them. Book One contains eight pieces, including the famous "Watchman's Song," "Fairy-Dance," and "National Song" – which was immediately set to stirring patriotic words by the influential Norwegian poet, playwright, and national hero, Bjørnstjerne Bjørnson, many of whose lyric verses Grieg later set to music.

Nina Grieg holding their baby daughter, Alexandra who died when she was just a year old. Edvard Grieg was profoundly affected by this loss, writing to his parents, "Our home has become empty.... I ask only for strength to work and accomplish something; then everything else will follow."

On April 10, 1868, Nina gave birth to a daughter named Alexandra. The family spent the summer in a cottage at Søllerød in Denmark, where Edvard composed one of his most famous works – the Piano Concerto in A minor. He had written relatively little for orchestra but embarked upon this major piece with youthful confidence and exuberance. From its striking opening – a downward cascade of chords for piano alone – to the lively folk dance rhythms of its finale, the Piano Concerto has come to stand for Norwegian music in many people's minds. It seems soaked in the clear mountain air, the melancholy wash of water in the fjords, and the traditions of a farming and fishing community.

A typical Norwegian landscape, with snow-capped mountains plunging into a fjord. Grieg's music is filled with the Norwegian mountain air which he loved so passionately.

After the death of their only child, Nina Grieg continued to work as a singer, giving the first performance of many of her husband's songs. Two of the most popular are settings of poems by Ibsen, "A Swan" and "With a Water-Lily."

Grief

When the summer ended, the Grieg family returned to Christiania, where Edvard grew increasingly depressed at his lack of prospects. After a long and bitterly cold winter, the baby Alexandra died when she was just over a year old. The Griegs' loss was extremely painful and they never had another child.

Now twenty-six, Edvard Grieg received a letter from the great pianist and composer Franz Liszt, who praised his compositions, and invited Grieg to visit him in Weimar in Austria. Such a testimonial from one of the most famous musicians of the time made Grieg's application for a grant to travel – which had at first been refused by the state – much easier. Meanwhile he laid plans for the first performance of the Piano Concerto in Copenhagen, and returned to his old family estate to spend the summer of 1869 composing. There he discovered a collection of Norwegian folk music, called *Mountain Melodies Old and New.*

Seized with enthusiasm, Grieg immediately made his own piano arrangements of twenty-five of these delightful Norwegian folk songs and dances –

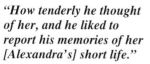

"How tenderly he thought of her, and he liked to report his memories of her [Alexandra's] short life."

Frank van der Strucken,
a friend of Grieg, 1883.

including "O the Pig Had a Snout," "Solfager and the Snake-King," "Said the Gadfly to the Fly," "Wedding Tune," and "Cow-Call Song" – and dedicated the collection to Ole Bull. From this time on, Grieg showed less interest in the large-scale forms of sonata or string quartet, and preferred to draw inspiration from this collection of folk melodies.

Meeting Liszt

In February 1870, the Griegs finally met Liszt, not in Weimar, but in Rome.

Grieg was intrigued by the aura which surrounded Liszt – then nearing sixty, his long hair white as snow, his nose covered in warts. In his youth, the golden-haired prodigy had been the idol of Europe, as famous for his notorious love affairs with aristocratic ladies as for his phenomenal keyboard technique. Five years before his meeting with the Griegs, Liszt had renounced his sensual existence for the simplicity of a cleric's life. He had left his current mistress, taken minor orders in the Catholic Church, and now wore the black gown of a priest

Franz Liszt was the most celebrated pianist in Europe. He was idolized by crowds wherever he went and was almost as famous for his many love-affairs as for his astonishing virtuoso piano playing. Grieg met Liszt in Rome in 1870, and wrote, "I brought him some of my compositions, which he played, and I was most interested to observe that it was the national element in them that caught his attention, and excited him."

(although he was never ordained). But despite this outward show of piety, the Griegs were puzzled to find the great man still permanently accompanied by an adoring entourage of young women, who gazed at Liszt "as if they would like to eat him, hide, hair, and all," and of languid young men, one of whom had even taken to wearing a copy of Liszt's clerical gown.

Liszt was intrigued by Grieg's Piano Concerto. He asked to see it and then immediately sat down to play it. He spoke encouraging words to Grieg who later talked about the experience saying, "the memory of this hour will have a wonderful power to sustain me in days of adversity."

First attempts at stage works

In 1873, Norway crowned a new king, Oscar II. To celebrate his coronation, several prominent citizens were knighted and Grieg was made a Knight of St. Olav for his services to Norwegian music. He was also awarded a grant for travel abroad to widen his musical horizons. In his application, Grieg stressed that part of the grant would be used to enable him to pursue "creative work in the dramatic field."

During the late nineteenth century, Norwegian drama was dominated by two giants, Bjørnstjerne Bjørnson and Henrik Ibsen. Grieg – as Norway's most successful nationalist composer – was closely involved with both men.

During the early 1870s he was preoccupied with the idea of writing an opera on a text by Bjørnson. He had already set some short texts by Bjørnson based on Norwegian folklore to music, and had provided incidental music, and background music of orchestral interludes, songs, and choruses, for Bjørnson's historical drama *Sigurd Jorsalfar*.

Now Bjørnson was pressing Grieg to finish a full-scale opera on the subject of the ancient king who introduced Christianity to Norway, *Olav Trygvason*. Grieg set to work on the small amount of text which Bjørnson had sent to him, but when no more was forthcoming he eventually lost interest in the project.

King Oscar II of Norway, who had a personal interest in music and was appointed foreign patron of the Royal Swedish Academy of music in 1873, the year he was also crowned King of Norway.

Then, Bjørnson heard that Grieg had accepted another commission, to compose music for Ibsen's play, *Peer Gynt*. He was furious, and broke off relations with Grieg – although he was increasingly turning away from nationalistic subjects anyway. It was probably this change of outlook which hindered Bjørnson's progress on *Olav Trygvason* although Grieg provided a convenient scapegoat.

Ibsen

Edvard Grieg had known Henrik Ibsen for many years. Ibsen had been contracted by Ole Bull to write and produce one play a year for the National Theater when it was first set up in 1849. Now Ibsen was in his mid-forties.

As a teenager Ibsen had begun to try his hand at a few plays, which brought him to the notice of Ole Bull. Bull appointed him playwright to the Norwegian Theater in Bergen, where between 1851 and 1857 he produced five dramas. In 1857 he moved to Christiania to take up a similar position as director of the Norwegian Theater there, but he encountered exactly the same public indifference as Grieg had, and his plays were not a success. In 1863 he received a scholarship to travel and went – like Grieg – to Rome, where he wrote the first of a series

Above: Henrik Ibsen, who first met Edvard Grieg when he was appointed playwright to the National Theater in Bergen. The two men first collaborated on Peer Gynt.
Left: A verse written by Ibsen in Grieg's album, when they were both in Rome in 1866,
"Orpheus with his wondrous tones
Roused souls in beasts, struck fire from stones.
Of stones has Norway not a few.
And beasts she has in plenty too.
Play then, that sparks from rocks may leap!
Play then, and pierce the brutes' hides deep!"

Opposite above: One of the original designs for the first production of Ibsen's play Peer Gynt, *the story of a thoughtless young hooligan who spends most of his life causing havoc among women. Grieg's music for the play contributed greatly to its initial success, and the two orchestral suites he later made from the music brought him money and fame.*

Opposite below: A troll, one of the ugly fairy-folk who are reputed to live in the Norwegian mountains. In Peer Gynt, *the hero is driven away from the Hall of the Mountain King by an army of trolls.*

of major plays which was to make him famous, *Brand*. It was followed a year later by *Peer Gynt*, which, in modern times, has established Ibsen's reputation as the greatest playwright of his time.

But he had had enough of the narrow outlook and lack of opportunities of Norway. After that he spent much of his time abroad in Italy or Germany, where his greatest plays – including *Pillars of Society, A Doll's House, Ghosts, The Wild Duck, Hedda Gabler,* and *The Master Builder* – were written. Ibsen was a master of social drama, and many of his plays tackle fundamental but controversial issues which were beginning to trouble late nineteenth century society, such as the role of women *(A Doll's House)* and the hereditary curse of venereal disease *(Ghosts)*.

Norwegian drama

One of the problems besetting a Norwegian dramatist of Ibsen's age was the lack of a national dramatic tradition. England, France, and Germany all had long traditions of spoken drama: English audiences from Elizabethan times onward happily sat through lengthy plays by William Shakespeare and his contemporaries. In France, the golden age of serious drama was the seventeenth century, when Corneille and Racine were writing their great verse dramas on ancient Greek or Roman subjects.

But Norwegians took a long time to accept the idea of spoken drama. When establishing his National Theater in Bergen, Ole Bull had encouraged playwrights to write musical plays, in which the dialogue was liberally sprinkled with songs and dances drawing on Norwegian folk culture. As dramas, these pieces were very slight, and audiences proved resistant to the idea of long, spoken plays without musical interludes to liven them up.

Peer Gynt

So, in 1874, when Ibsen was planning a production of his verse drama *Peer Gynt* in Christiania, he asked Grieg if he would supply some incidental music to accompany the play.

Peer Gynt is about a young man in Norway who abandons his faithful girlfriend, Solveig, then abducts a bride at a wedding feast, only to leave her in the mountains. He then roams the rocky mountains, flirting shamelessly with dairy-maids on his way, until he reaches the domains of the Mountain King of the Dovre, a range of mountains in central Norway. Peer Gynt then falls in love with the Mountain King's daughter, but is driven away from the castle by a furious army of trolls. He returns home to find his mother dying, and sets out

again to make his fortune abroad. After many years, now a rich man, he finds his way to the North African desert, where he meets the daughter of a Bedouin chief, Anitra. Their brief affair reminds Peer of his first love, Solveig, who has patiently waited for his return all this time. At last, as a weary old man, Peer is shipwrecked on the Norwegian coast, and is reunited with Solveig.

Ibsen asked Grieg to provide dance music for the wedding scene in Act One, harmonies to accompany Peer Gynt's speeches, songs for Solveig and the exotic Anitra, and music to accompany the scene with the Old Man of the Dovre (now known as "In the Hall of the Mountain King").

Grieg accepted the commission and started working on the project but he found the task difficult – the play, according to him, was "a very unmusical subject." In August 1874 he told a friend about the problems he was having, "*Peer Gynt*

"Norwegian everyday life, Norwegian sagas and history, and above all Norwegian scenery have exercized a strong influence on my creative work ever since my youth."

Edvard Grieg, letter to American biographer H.T. Finck, July 1900.

progresses very slowly, and there is no possibility of getting it finished by autumn. It is a terribly unmanageable subject."

In the end, against his earlier expectations, Grieg produced over twenty musical numbers. Act One is mostly taken up with wedding music, including the traditional dances *halling* and *springdans,* played by solo violin in traditional Hardanger fiddle style.

Act Two describes Peer's grotesque encounter with the trolls, including the episode in the Dovre King's hall (which became one of Grieg's best-known pieces). Act Three introduces Solveig, who sings as she waits patiently for Peer's return, and ends with the death of Åse. Act Four opens with the piece now normally referred to as "Morning." Peer Gynt encounters the sultry Anitra in the Moroccan desert (her sensuous dance is scored for strings and triangle alone). In Act Five, Peer finally returns home to Norway. The play ends with Solveig's lullaby.

A scene from Peer Gynt. *Here Peer is shown enticing the young bride away from her own wedding reception He later abandons her in the mountains.*

The success of *Peer Gynt*

Peer Gynt was first performed in Christiania on February 28, 1876. It was a huge success, and Grieg went on to put together two orchestral suites from the music, which include all its most famous numbers. This quickly became as famous as the play itself, and, like the play, became renowned in its own right.

At the time, both Grieg and Ibsen were highly acclaimed for the success of *Peer Gynt*. Grieg's naturally sunny temperament helped him get along with the prickly, difficult Ibsen, and the two became friends. A young poet from Bergen, John Paulsen, wrote of his meeting with both men, "Ibsen was ... unapproachable throughout the day. He often invited me to go on walks, but didn't speak a word.... Nonetheless, when we parted he never failed to thank me for my 'pleasant company'.... In the

A scene from a modern production of Peer Gynt *showing how modern costume and setting can lend itself to the portrayal of the play.*

evening, however, he usually loosened up and became talkative and jovial. Grieg had a special ability to get him going ... I cannot recall Ibsen ever using an enthusiastic expression...."

In 1875 Grieg had set six poems by Ibsen, including the famous "A Swan," and "With a Waterlily," which Nina Grieg had often sang in her recitals. He dearly wanted to compose an opera to a libretto by Ibsen, but the collaboration never materialized. Ten years later, Grieg regretfully accepted that "the Norwegian drama in Norwegian music which I have dreamt of, which I always believed I could create one day ... is fated to come from another."

> *"Before long it may well be that Ibsen's* **Peer Gynt** *will continue to live only through Grieg's music, for so far as I am concerned this music contains in each of its movements more poetry and artistic insight than all five acts of Ibsen's play put together."*
> *Eduard Hanslick,*
> *Vienna critic, 1891.*

In the mountains

After the excitement of *Peer Gynt*, Grieg, now thirty-four, settled back into his routine of rehearsals, choir practices, and giving piano lessons. He and Nina

Edvard Grieg's composing hut at Troldhaugen. He preferred to work in a small cabin away from the main house, and surrounded by the sounds and sights of nature.

decided to spend the summer of 1877 in the mountainous and beautiful Hardanger district, just inland from Bergen. They took lodgings on a farm at first, and then moved to the guesthouse at Lofthus on the Sørfjord, run by Hans and Brita Utne and their twelve children.

Grieg took over the village schoolroom for his work as there was no school during the summer, but then moved down to a tiny log hut by the water's edge. When he was continually distracted by passers-by there, he persuaded fifty sturdy villagers to haul the hut bodily halfway up the mountain, to a more peaceful spot. There he wrote his String Quartet in G minor, a work which "aims at breadth, vitality, and above all, at bringing out the sound of the instruments for which it is written."

Ballads

Edvard Grieg also turned back for inspiration to collections of folk poetry, where, among many other verses he set to music that summer, he found the words of a ballad called *The Mountain Thrall*. He claimed that his fine, strongly nationalistic setting of these words, for solo male singer, two horns, and strings, was very close to his heart.

A Norwegian peasant in the dress of the Hardanger district. Fur-lined boots like these were essential wear for the long, freezing winters.

Other songs were in the rural Norwegian dialect, *landsmål*, a form of speech shunned by many educated Norwegians, who associated it with ignorant peasants. Among Grieg's settings in this dialect are the songs "The Spring" and "The Wounded Heart."

Grieg was happy among his beloved mountains. For his thirty-fifth birthday, he and Nina gave a party to which both Ole Bull and a famous local fiddler, Ola Mosafinn, were both invited, and who entertained the guests with their wild, passionate fiddling.

Travels

For the next few years, Grieg divided his time between Hardanger and concert tours – and this time away from home began to put a strain on his marriage. In the winter of 1878 he revisited Leipzig. Now he was a famous composer rather than an unhappy student and his String Quartet, F major Violin Sonata, and the Piano Concerto were all well received.

In 1879 he was made conductor of the Bergen Harmonic Society – a post he accepted out of duty, but disliked. He felt that the orchestra was totally incompetent and the administrators obstructive. Rather unwillingly, Grieg battled against "stupidity and abuse" for two years.

Finding it increasingly difficult to compose, Grieg urged himself into action by signing a deal with his publisher in which, in return for an annual fee, he agreed to produce a certain amount of new music

"I sought peace, insight, and self-understanding, and all of this I found in the magnificent Hardanger district. The place became so dear to me that for four to five years I continued to go back every summer."

Edvard Grieg, in a letter to
G. Schjelderup, September, 1903.

39

every year. The first of these compositions, a cello sonata, was dispatched in 1883, but a promised second piano concerto never materialized.

Marriage problems

Instead, Grieg's publisher received a steady stream of *Lyric Pieces* for solo piano: between 1883 and 1901 nine more volumes appeared, containing such much-loved gems as "Butterfly," "To the Spring," "Little Bird," "Shepherd Boy," and "Trolls' March."

In 1883 Grieg paid his second visit to Bayreuth, in Bavaria, where a hall had been specially built by the famous opera composer, Richard Wagner to put on his massive music-dramas. Grieg then took a prolonged tour of central Germany – including Dresden and Weimar, and Holland. During all these months, Nina was left at home, and Grieg is said to have had a relationship with a young Norwegian painter, Elise Schjelderup, who lived mainly in Paris.

Suddenly, matters came to a head. Grieg was exhausted by the physical and emotional demands of his work, combined with this love affair. Frants Beyer, one of his closest Bergen friends, managed to reconcile Grieg with Nina, who joined him in

The music room at Troldhaugen. In these surroundings, Grieg was able to find expression for his creativity, "To write music depicting Norwegian scenery, the life of the people, the country's history, and folk poetry appears to me to be a calling in which I feel I could achieve something."

Amsterdam, before the pair set off together to spend the winter in Italy. In Rome, they met Ibsen again, and Nina sang Grieg's settings of his poems. After she had finished "A Swan," Grieg said, "the ice-crust melted, and he [Ibsen] came over to the piano … with tears in his eyes … without being able to say a word. He mumbled something to the effect that this was 'understanding'…."

Troldhaugen

Edvard and Nina returned to Bergen in the spring of 1884, determined to make a success of their marriage. Their good friends the Beyers had built themselves a brand new house on a promontory overlooking a lake just south of Bergen. The Griegs decided that this was an ideal spot to make their own summer home, and they bought a plot of land on the other side of the lake – they and the Beyers could row across to visit each other.

During the summer, which they spent in Hardanger, Edvard and Nina planned their new home. Just below the little hill where it would be built was a hollow called "Trolldalen" (The Valley of the Trolls), and Nina decided that the new house would be called "Troldhaugen" (The Hill of the Trolls). It was an ideal place, with a wonderful view, and close enough to the mountains for Grieg and his friends to go on long walking tours, which he loved.

The villa that Edvard and Nina built in 1885 when they were in their early forties, at Troldhaugen (the Hill of the Trolls), where they spent many summers.

41

The young Frederick Delius whom Grieg first met in 1887. Delius was strongly attracted to Edvard Grieg's music and to the scenery of Norway, and the two men became close friends. Between 1888 and the end of Grieg's life they kept a lively correspondence.

By April 1885, the house was ready for occupancy. It would be Grieg's home – at least during the summer months – for the rest of his life, and although the expense of building it caused him financial worries, he was never happier than when out for a quiet morning in his boat, rowing up the fjord between the skerries, or islands, and the cliffs.

New friends

In 1886, the Griegs were visited at Troldhaugen by a young Italian violinist, Teresina Tua. Grieg, much smitten with her, called her "my little fiddle-fairy on my troll-hill," and, inspired by her playing, began work on a third violin sonata.

This lyrical work, full of memorable tunes and luscious harmonies, was first performed in Leipzig in December of the following year. There, at this time, the Griegs first met a twenty-five year old student at the Conservatory, who was to become one of their closest friends, Frederick Delius.

Delius, whose father owned a wool-making mill in England, was familiar with Scandinavia. His father had sent him to Sweden on business five years earlier, and he could already speak fluent Norwegian and Swedish. Delius had fallen passionately in love with the majestic beauty of the Norwegian countryside, and instead of making trade contacts, as

To travel by carriage was the main method of transport in Norway, as shown in this picture of 1880s. At this time the roads were quite dangerous and would be impassable during winter. Edvard Grieg often used a stolkjerre *or small two-wheeled carriage to make his journeys across the country.*

his father wished, and getting on with the business of selling wool, he spent his time visiting the snow-capped mountains, the rushing waterfalls, and the ice-cold, bottomless fjords.

This unworldly attitude brought Frederick Delius into conflict with his father, and after a series of bitter arguments, he left the family business to go to the United States to try his hand at orange growing. He crossed the Atlantic in 1884, but failed to make a success of his new trade. Instead he became a piano teacher. By this time his father had given up on him, and when friends urged him to go to Leipzig to pursue his first love – music – his father finally gave way. In 1886, Frederick Delius started studying at the Leipzig Conservatory.

Grieg and Delius

At the Conservatory, Delius quickly made friends with two other young Norwegian musicians, Sinding and Halvorsen. When Edvard and Nina Grieg visited Leipzig Johan Halvorsen played Grieg's new violin sonata through "with such warmth and genuine artistry that I had a fit of pride at his being a countryman of mine," Grieg remembered. The Griegs soon saw a lot of Halvorsen and Sinding and they often relaxed together after lunch.

Just after the first performance of Grieg's new sonata, Delius was introduced to Edvard and Nina Grieg. Delius recalled, "During my stay in Leipzig, I had become great friends with Christian Sinding, the Norwegian composer, and we always took our midday meal together at the Panorama Restaurant. One day on our way thither suddenly Sinding said to me, 'There's Mr. and Mrs. Grieg' and I saw coming toward us two quite small people... I saw a little man with a broad-brimmed hat and long hair and on his arm a little woman with hair cut quite short. I was speedily introduced. We all four then made our way to the Panorama Restaurant to have dinner. I was very proud at having made his acquaintance, for since I was a little boy I had loved his music ... when I first heard Grieg it was as if a breath of fresh mountain air had come to me.

"...a man who can enthuse over a genius like Grieg is much more than a musical critic: He is a music lover."

Frederick Delius, in a letter to Percy Grainger, 1924.

"Grieg, learning how well I knew Norway and hearing that I had just returned from a mountain tour, naturally took great interest in me and we soon found ourselves comparing notes of mountain trips in Jotunheimen and the Hardanger Vidder."

Christmas celebrations

Grieg was very taken with the enthusiastic, impulsive Englishman, whom he called the "Hardangerviddeman," and they became strong friends. He invited Delius, Sinding, and Halvorsen to his lodgings for Christmas Eve, which was to be enlivened by a hamper of fine wines. Nina sang some of Edvard's songs; Halvorsen played the G major Violin Sonata with Grieg at the piano, and Delius played his own piece, "A Norwegian Sleigh-Ride."

As the evening wore on everyone became, as Grieg put it, "completely plastered." A Christmas tree with lighted candles stood on the piano, and during the evening the candles set the tree on fire. Sinding scrambled up onto the piano to put out the blaze, and knocked the whole thing over. By that time, all the four of them could do was roar helplessly with laughter. "What a Christmas Eve!" wrote Grieg. "We broke up at half past two."

London

Edvard Grieg, forty-five years old and well known as Norway's foremost composer, was receiving more invitations than he could cope with. In 1888 he visited London, England, twice. At a concert on the first occasion he played his Piano Concerto and "The Last Spring", which, according to him, "sounded as if the whole of Nature was calling to me from home; I felt proud and glad to be Norwegian." Grieg received a standing ovation from the packed house. Grieg returned to England in August, to conduct his own works – including the string version of the *Holberg Suite*.

In the spring of 1889 Grieg returned to England once more and his *Elegiac Melodies* were played along with the Piano Concerto. He also gave a series of recitals at which all three of his violin sonatas were played.

Then, having conquered England, he decided to try his luck with the unpredictable Paris public,

"To have the ability to withdraw into oneself and forget <u>everything</u> around one when one is creating – that, I think, is the only requirement for being able to bring forth something beautiful. The whole thing is – a mystery."
Edvard Grieg,
in a letter to Agathe Backer
Grondahl, November, 1905.

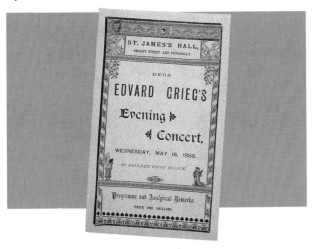

In 1888 Edvard Grieg paid his first visit to England. This was his first concert there in London on May 16, 1888. He played his own Piano Concerto, and the concert was a great success.

45

playing pieces that he felt comfortable with – the *Peer Gynt* suites and the Piano Concerto. Once again, Grieg was a great success.

Walks in the Jotunheim

Between these exhausting concert tours, Grieg returned every summer to Troldhaugen and the mountains, where, dressed in thick walking clothes, a felt hat, and gaiters, he sallied forth in all weathers.

In the summer of 1889, he was joined by Delius and Sinding, and they went on a walking tour, staying in a tiny hut high up in the Jotunheim Mountains, on the lakeside. Here, according to Delius, "we spent a very pleasant time, fishing, boating, walking. Our principal food was trout from the lake, wonderful trout. Milk we got from a *saeter* (a hill farm) on the other side of the lake a few miles away. We ate *flatbrod,* the flat Norwegian oatcakes, and every evening we had hot whisky toddy and played cards."

On another excursion into the Jotunheim the following summer, another of Grieg's houseguests, the Dutch musician Julius Röntgen, described how the party heard farm girls singing genuine folk songs while they milked their cows, and another woman sang a lullaby to a newborn baby, and then played a haunting farewell on a goat-horn.

An oratorio for peace

In 1890 Grieg tried to re-establish his former collaboration with the playwright Bjørnson, suggesting that they write an oratorio on the subject of peace. That subject was very much on everyone's minds in the 1890s, since Sweden, which dealt with Norway's foreign affairs, was becoming alarmed by Norwegian nationalism, and was threatening to suspend Norway's constitution. The situation became increasingly tense throughout the 1890s, and the two states were on the brink of war, until their crowns were formally separated in 1905.

Bjørnson responded with enthusiasm, but then produced a text dealing not, as Grieg had hoped, with abstract ideals, but with issues of contemporary life. Grieg simply did not possess either the temperament or the musical vocabulary to cope with this modern approach, and the idea was dropped.

Silver wedding day at Troldhaugen

Both Grieg and Röntgen put the songs they had heard in the Jotunheim to good use – Grieg in a piano piece and Röntgen in a suite for violin and piano, which he gave to Nina and Edvard for their twenty-fifth wedding anniversary. This they celebrated at Troldhaugen on June 11, 1892.

The festivities began at dawn with a military band. Then the couple received presents, including a new Steinway grand piano from the town of Bergen, a portrait from Christiania, and a silver sugar bowl filled with gold pieces from a publisher in Leipzig.

Over one hundred guests arrived and were invited to stay for dinner. In the evening, the sky was lit up with fireworks and bonfires. All around the lake – watching from the hillsides, or rowing in boats – thousands of people came to share the festive atmosphere, and Grieg played the "Wedding Day at Troldhaugen" on the new Steinway to commemorate the occasion.

Too popular?

By the 1890s, Edvard Grieg felt that he had reached a turning point. His music was popular and widely accepted, but he felt that his fame rested only on his early works – the Piano Concerto, *Peer Gynt,* and the *Lyric Pieces* – and he felt the need to expand his horizons. He also suffered the fate of many popular composers in the form of unkind gibes from critics who considered his music lightweight. The Irish playwright, Bernard Shaw called Grieg "a musical grasshopper," and the French composer Claude Debussy memorably characterized his music as "leaving in the mouth the taste of a pink sweetie stuffed with snow."

Near the end of his life, Grieg complained of his excessive popularity, which was a problem for him

"[Grieg] is nothing more than a clever musician, one who is more concerned about mere effects than true art."
Claude Debussy
in Gil Blas, April, 1903.

The scenery in Telemark, in southern Norway, painted in the late nineteenth century by the Norwegian artist, Skramstad. This is the kind of country which Edvard Grieg would have often seen on his many walking tours.

in his search for perfection, "I can tell you that I have quite a burden resting on my weak shoulders – the task of arousing an awareness of the ideal in music. But it is wonderful to have a mission in life, and that I have. It demands a willingness to make sacrifices, that's for sure, but there are moments when I experience a truly radiant joy."

Illness

Shortly after the Griegs celebrated their twenty-fifth wedding anniversary, Edvard became unwell with stomach and lung trouble. Nina dreaded having to spend the freezing winters in Troldhaugen, and was probably rather less fond of the district than Edvard was. She never accompanied him on his long walking tours, and actually much preferred the milder climate of Denmark, where she had grown up. She was frantic with worry. He recovered, however, and the couple left for Copenhagen and then for Leipzig, planning to spend the spring on the French Riviera, where the warmth and sun would benefit Edvard's health.

Nina wrote to Delius, "You know how wonderful it is here ... how the ... olive groves hang down like a veil from the rocks, how the soft air is full of the fragrance of blossoms.... Unfortunately I have to enjoy all this too much on my own, firstly Grieg is ill, secondly his mind is too full of the Jotunfjelde and all of Norwegian nature."

Meanwhile Grieg had been offered an honorary doctorate by the University of Cambridge, England, but he was not strong enough to travel. Instead, he and Nina returned to Norway where a doctor prescribed pine baths and massage at a spa resort.

In the summer of 1893 Grieg and Röntgen set off again on another walking trip in the Jotunheim, but Grieg was again unwell and they had to return to Troldhaugen quickly.

Edvard Grieg dressed for walking. He was described by an English visitor, the Rev. W. W. Gray, "His figure, even shorter and slighter than I first imagined it to be, was encased in a tight-fitting ulster and gaiters; his thick hair, just turning white, fell down on his collar from beneath a felt hat; and ulster, gaiters, and hat alike bore traces of mountain walks and mountain weather..."

The spring of song

That winter it was Nina, now forty-eight, who suffered a kidney complaint and spent six weeks being looked after. Concern for his wife's health – and the possibility of losing her – roused Grieg to another wave of creative activity in the form of "a mass of songs."

The three volumes that resulted were all settings of Norwegian texts: *Norway* and *Elegiac Poems*, and *Poems by Vilhelm Krag* (a young poet from southern Norway), followed by *Children's Songs* later in the year. Within another year, Grieg followed these with another collection of settings of *landsmål* poems by Arne Garborg, *Haugtussa*, which were to be his last important songs.

As well as another four books of *Lyric Pieces* (the eighth set contains the famous "Wedding Day at Troldhaugen"), Grieg's piano compositions of the 1890s were all strongly nationalistic in character.

The *Symphonic Dances* for piano duet, the *Old Norwegian Melody with Variations* for two pianos, which was inspired by Robert Schumann; and the *Nineteen Norwegian Folk Tunes* were based on tunes collected during his tours of the Jotunheim.

Slåtter

Grieg's next important composition – also for piano – was a set of Norwegian folk dance tunes, which he transcribed from the playing of an old Hardanger fiddle virtuoso, Knut Dale.

Dale had first contacted Grieg in 1888, asking if he would be interested in saving these tunes, and in 1901 Grieg enlisted the help of the violinist Johann Halvorsen. Halvorsen was now a conductor of the orchestra in Christiania and Grieg contacted him because he felt that "only a violinist with a feeling for the Norwegian spirit" could note the music down accurately.

Halvorsen did not find the task an easy one. He told Grieg that "there are small turns and trills like a little trout in a rapid [that] are the life and soul of the *slåtter*, they … have the effect of a kind of 'quivering'." Halvorsen also told Grieg that in tunes in the key of D major, there was nearly always a G sharp (known as the interval of an augmented fourth) which gave the pieces their characteristic Norwegian sound. Grieg replied that "the augmented fourth can also be heard in peasants' songs." Grieg's piano transcriptions of seventeen of these dance tunes, or *slåtter,* were finally published in 1903.

Routine

For the next twenty years, Edvard Grieg's routine remained much the same – concert tours followed by summers relaxing at Troldhaugen in Norway.

As he got older, he found the touring schedule increasingly arduous – sea crossings in the small, cramped steamers of those days were not to be undertaken lightly (especially in the rough North Sea), and he suffered from the cold, damp weather in places like England, where he complained about the perpetual fog.

In spring 1894, Grieg was in Paris. There he met the nineteen year old Maurice Ravel, then a student at the Paris Conservatoire, but later to become one of France's most important composers of the early twentieth century.

Ravel had played Grieg's Piano Concerto for one of his Conservatoire exams, and at a party given for Grieg, Ravel began to play one of the composer's dances. Grieg listened attentively, and then told Ravel to make the rhythm of this peasant dance more marked. "You should see the peasants at home with the fiddler stamping time with his foot," he cried. "Play it again!" And then, to the astonishment of the company, Grieg began to demonstrate the steps of the dance, hopping and skipping around the room in time to the music. Later Ravel was heard to agree that modern French music owed much to the influence of Grieg.

"Grieg's music at its best is so fresh, poetic and original – in fact, just like Norway."
Frederick Delius from Grieg and Delius A Chronicle of Their Friendship in Letters.

Rebel

In May that year, Grieg finally made it to England to receive his doctorate from Cambridge University. He found the solemnity of the whole affair absurd. "I could have died laughing," he told a friend later. "Costume: blue and white gown, medieval cap. Scene: a festively decorated street. Action: procession through the town."

Immediately after that he became seriously unwell, and had to return to a spa town near Christiania for treatment before going back to Troldhaugen. He spent the winter in Denmark, where his health continued to worsen and in March 1895 he caught pneumonia.

Grieg's fragile state did not prevent him from falling in love again, this time with a young Danish pianist, Bella Edwards. But he and Nina were still together that winter in Leipzig, where Nina had to undergo hospital treatment for suspected breast cancer. Grieg had to leave her there while he made the journey to Vienna to give a concert of his own works. She recovered and, in April 1896, they returned to Norway, stopping in Copenhagen on the way for Edvard to conduct the Berlin Philharmonic Orchestra in a performance of his Piano Concerto.

The French composer Maurice Ravel, whom Edvard Grieg met in Paris in 1894, when Ravel was only nineteen and still a student. Ravel went on to become one of the most important French composers of the early twentieth century.

Meeting with a queen

In late 1897 Grieg visited England again, conducting ten concerts within the space of a month. Early in December he and Nina were granted an audience by the widowed Queen Victoria, then nearing the end of her long reign. The Queen – who as a young woman was married to a music-loving German prince and much enjoyed the music of Mendelssohn – was kindly disposed toward talented foreign composers, and knew Grieg's music. "The Queen is *sweet*, if one can say this about an elderly lady," wrote Grieg. "She knew almost the entire programme, *enjoyed* Nina's singing in Norwegian, and asked for more.... She is so charming and interesting, quite astonishingly so for an old lady."

On this occasion, Grieg also made a tour of the Netherlands, where he was treated like a king

Queen Victoria of England gave Grieg a private audience of his music. Although he was never impressed by authority, the composer took an instant liking to the queen, whom he found "natural and genuine."

himself. In Amsterdam he heard the world-famous Concertgebouw Orchestra conducted by the great Willem Mengelberg. The experience left such a strong impression on Grieg that the following year, when asked to take part in organizing a national music festival in Bergen, he invited the Concertgebouw Orchestra without consulting the other members of the festival committee.

Snubbing his country

Although Norway only possessed one professional orchestra – the Christiania Musical Society, which could not begin to approach the standard of the brilliant Amsterdam orchestra – the Norwegians felt they had been snubbed, and were deeply offended. To save this embarrassing situation, it was agreed to hire an amateur Festival Chorus and to engage professional Norwegian soloists.

In the end, the Bergen Festival was a great success and a personal triumph for Grieg. The Amsterdam Concertgebouw Orchestra arrived on the Stavanger ferry, from where a specially chartered boat took them up the Hardanger fjord to Eide. Then they went in a fleet of horse-drawn carriages to the station at Vossevangen, and finally arrived in Bergen by train. The Norwegians swallowed their national pride and

"In Grieg's own playing there is both power and a marvellous confidence, and above all there is a lucidity that allows none of the music's beauty to escape the notice of anyone who listens attentively to his performance."

From Aftenbladet, *October, 1866.*

*"The Opera Orchestra"
by the French artist
Edgar Degas, painted in
the late 1860s.
Orchestras in Grieg's
time would have looked
like this.*

entertained the Dutch orchestra royally. Most people had never heard such amazing orchestral playing in their lives. "You should have seen the countryfolk, who had come from far and wide, and stood there during the wonderful pianissimos of the string orchestra, as reverently as if they were in church, while the tears streamed down their faces," wrote Grieg enthusiastically.

At the end of the festival, the orchestra was given a triumphant send-off, accompanied down to the quayside at Bergen by a crowd of over ten thousand people and a military band.

The Dreyfus case

The success of the Bergen Festival raised the profile of Norwegian music and persuaded the government to take more of an interest in its national art.

In 1899 a new National Theater opened in

Christiania, with its own professional symphony orchestra, which was subsidized financially by the city. One of the opening plays there was Bjørnson's *Sigurd Jorsalfar*, with incidental music by Grieg. After conducting the performance, the Griegs went to stay with the Bjørnsons – and became involved in a fierce political argument.

A French army officer named Alfred Dreyfus had been tried by a military tribunal and condemned to public humiliation and life imprisonment for allegedly spying for the Germans. Dreyfus was Jewish, and many people believed that he was innocent, but had been framed by some anti-Jewish fellow officers. Dreyfus was sent to the dreaded prison camp on Devil's Island. In 1898, the great French writer Émile Zola issued his famous pamphlet *J'accuse!*, accusing the government of a terrible miscarriage of justice.

A year later, it finally emerged that the documents which convicted Dreyfus had been forged. He was released – a broken man – while the French army officer, who had really been guilty, committed suicide.

Le capitaine Dreyfus devant le conseil de guerre

Making a stand

At the time of the Griegs' visit to the Bjørnsons, the Dreyfus Case was raging, and intellectuals all over Europe – among them the Bjørnsons – were firmly on the side of Dreyfus.

It so happened that just at that time, Grieg had received an invitation to go to Paris to conduct a series of concerts. Influenced by the strongly held views of his friends (although he himself rarely got involved in politics), Grieg immediately sat down and wrote a letter refusing the invitation. His letter was published widely in many European newspapers and, while many people praised him for his courageous stand against injustice, he received hate mail from France, where feelings were running high, threatening that if he showed his face in Paris again, he would be "kicked in the backside."

Grieg avoided Paris for another three years, by which time he hoped that the affair would be completely forgotten.

Alfred Dreyfus, the French Jewish officer wrongfully accused in 1894 of spying for the Germans, stands at his military trial, as it appeared in Le Petit Journal, *a newspaper of the time. The "Dreyfus Case" tore Europe apart as everyone took sides, and Grieg himself became embroiled. He refused an invitation to Paris on principle, and when he did visit to conduct a concert three years later, he had to be protected by the police.*

Visit to Paris

In April 1903, fifty-nine year old Edvard Grieg went to Paris to conduct a series of concerts that included a selection of his own works, among them the Piano Concerto, the first *Peer Gynt* Suite, "Solveig's Song," and other orchestral works. An audience of almost four thousand came to hear and see Grieg and an extra-large contingent of police had been drafted in case of trouble. A noisy group of demonstrators tried to wreck the concert by whistling and jeering, but were removed by the police.

Later the Griegs were escorted back to their hotel by the police. "I had taken five drops of opium," Grieg told a friend later, "which had a remarkably calming effect on me." One critic much later recalled him at rehearsal "leaping up the tiered rostra to verify a note in the trombone part, as nimble as [an] elf."

The concert was a great success, but the composer and music critic Claude Debussy – also France's greatest twentieth century musician – said that Grieg's "sweet, pale" songs were only of use "to lull ladies to sleep... there always seems to be one note that drags over a chord, like a water lily on a lake whose flower is tired of being watched by the moon..." and complained that the Piano Concerto had nothing original about it, but owed a great deal to Schumann. The otherwise all-Grieg concert had ended with some excerpts from Wagner's opera *Götterdämmerung,* which Debussy found extraordinary saying, "You don't eat roast beef after little sweetmeats."

Birthday celebrations

Nineteen hundred and three was Edvard Grieg's last really busy year. Apart from Paris, he also visited Warsaw and Prague, where he was welcomed with wide acclaim.

By mid-June he was back in Troldhaugen in time to celebrate his sixtieth birthday. The week-long celebrations included a reception at Troldhaugen, an official banquet in the Grand Hotel in Bergen, and concerts by the National Theater orchestra. Grieg –

with typical generosity and extravagance – arranged for the entire orchestra to be transported up in horse-drawn carriages to one of the mountains surrounding Bergen, where everyone was treated to lunch and they then performed an open-air concert. But, as Grieg wrote to Delius, "[later] came the reaction.... Since the end of June I have been seriously ill.... The festival with concerts and banquets was beyond my strength."

Later that year, he wrote a similar letter to Delius saying that he had "arrived at that stage in life where I could no longer write 'A Dance of Life', but only 'Weariness of Life'.... "

Sixtieth birthday celebrations at Troldhaugen. Although he enjoyed peace and quiet, Grieg also loved the company of other people and particularly enjoyed entertaining them at his idyllic home.

Partial recovery

But by the following spring, Grieg had recovered enough to make a concert tour of Sweden. During the summer, which he spent at Troldhaugen, he was invited to breakfast with the German Kaiser, Wilhelm II, who kept his yacht moored in Bergen. Grieg – always a man of proud and independent temperament – disliked bowing and scraping to royalty, and was reluctant to accept, but he found the kaiser "a human being and not an Emperor."

Wilhelm II, emperor of Germany in Grieg's time. The kaiser is chiefly remembered now for having dragged his country – and the whole of Europe – into the horrors of World War I, but he was a cultured man who kept his own private orchestra, and loved music, poetry, and painting. He impressed Grieg far more than his uncle, King Edward VII of England.

During breakfast they discussed not only music, but many other subjects, including "poetry, painting, religion, socialism and God knows what else." Then, to Grieg's great surprise, the kaiser summoned his own private forty-piece orchestra to give a concert of Grieg's works, during which Grieg was much amused to see the German monarch illustrating "the effect of the music by movements of the head and body. *Anitra's Dance* quite electrified him, it was marvellous to see his serpentine convolutions in the manner of an Oriental maiden."

The two men met again the following evening, and Grieg summed up the kaiser as "a strange mixture of great energy, great self-confidence, and great kindness of heart."

Interrupting

Grieg was less impressed two years later, when, during the course of his last tour of England in the spring of 1906, he was asked to give a command performance in front of England's Edward VII and Queen Alexandra. The king – no great music lover – talked so loudly all the way through that Grieg had to stop playing twice. Later he complained to Edward's son-in-law, the new king of Norway, who tried to excuse his royal relative by saying he was the sort of person who could easily listen to music and talk at the same time. Grieg retorted, "That may well be possible, but all the same it is not permissible, even for the King of England, and in justice to my art I cannot overlook it." King Haakon of Norway just smiled and shrugged.

During that visit to London, Grieg met an excitable young Australian composer and pianist, Percy Grainger. Grainger was a great friend of Delius' and he turned the pages for Grieg at a recital. Nina and Edvard left a lasting impression on Percy Grainger, as a couple who "are so completely happy together and both so loveable and kind."

Later Percy, Edvard and Nina, were invited to lunch with the new Norwegian ambassador to London, to celebrate the first National Constitution Day, as Norway had achieved its independence from

Percy Grainger, the Australian-born pianist, composer, and collector of English and Scandinavian folk-music, became a close friend of Grieg's near the end of the Norwegian composer's life. Grieg thought that Grainger was the ideal performer of his piano music.

Sweden in 1905. On May 29, 1906, Edvard, aged sixty-three, received another degree, this time from the prestigious Oxford University in England.

Relapse

Unable to face a winter suffering from the darkness and bitter winds of western Norway and in failing health, Edvard Grieg chose to spend the winter of 1906 at a hotel in Christiania. Here he completed his last work, *Four Psalms,* for mixed chorus.

Although weakened, Grieg managed to complete another tour in the spring of 1907. This time he visited Copenhagen, Munich, Kiel, and Berlin, returning to Denmark at the end of April for a course of hydrotherapy. By this time, his ever-present lung disease was rapidly taking its toll.

In the summer of 1907, the Griegs were joined for the last time at Troldhaugen by Julius Röntgen and Percy Grainger, who was to play Grieg's Piano Concerto later in the year in England. Grainger and Grieg spent much time going over the solo part and making small alterations. "You have become for me," he wrote to Grainger later, "a dear young friend who has enriched the evening of my life." Grainger's performance of the Grieg Concerto was preserved on a piano roll (the forerunner of recordings).

Last moments

Grieg intended to go to Grainger's performance of the Concerto, and on September 2, he and Nina set out for Bergen, intending to take a boat for England the following morning. But that night he was unwell at his hotel and taken to Bergen Hospital, where he sank into a coma.

Edvard Grieg died on the morning of September 4, 1907, aged sixty-four. Between forty and fifty thousand people were estimated to have watched his funeral procession pass through the streets of Bergen, and an orchestra played the Funeral March that he had written for Rikaard Nordraak and "The Last Spring" at his graveside. His ashes were placed in a grotto in the cliff overlooking the fjord at his beloved Troldhaugen – the perfect resting place for Norway's most famous composer.

Below: Grieg in his final years and (right) his portrait on a stamp to commemorate his life. Despite having achieved such worldwide renown, Grieg never looked for fame. After his death Nina Grieg referred to her husband's real interests, "First and foremost, he was a good and honorable person – that was most important to him – and then the good genuine artist. He was a friend of humanity."

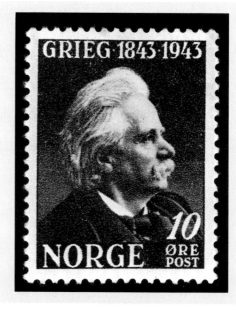

GRIEG·1843·1943

10

NORGE ØRE POST

Important Dates

1843   June 15: Edvard Grieg is born in the Norwegian port of Bergen.

1858   Ole Bull visits the Griegs and recommends that Edvard should be sent to study in Leipzig.
October: Edvard, aged fifteen, enters the Leipzig Conservatory.

1860   Edvard has to spend the summer at home recovering from a severe lung infection.

1862   April: Nineteen year old Grieg graduates from Leipzig with glowing reports from his teachers.

1863   Edvard moves to the Danish capital Copenhagen, the main city for culture in Scandinavia, and meets the Danish composer Niels Gade and half-Norwegian composer and pianist Rikard Nordraak.

1864   Grieg, aged twenty, meets his cousin Nina Hagerup, aged eighteen. In July they become engaged.

1865   Grieg and Nordraak travel to Italy, where Grieg writes *Humoreskes* for piano, and other sonatas for piano and violin.

1866   Nordraak dies in Berlin. Grieg writes the Funeral March in his memory.
Grieg moves to the capital of Norway, Christiania.

1867   Edvard Grieg and Nina Hagerup are married. Grieg becomes conductor of the amateur Christiania Philharmonic Society. He writes Book One of *Lyric Pieces*.

1868   April 10: Nina gives birth to the Griegs' first and only child, Alexandra.
Grieg writes his Piano Concerto.

1869   After a long, cold winter, Alexandra dies. Grieg discovers an important collection of Norwegian folk-music.

1870   On invitation, Grieg meets the world-famous pianist, Liszt, in Rome. He writes *Norwegian Dances and Songs* and begins working with the dramatist, Björnson.

1873   Grieg is made a Knight of St. Olav for his contribution to Norwegian music. He begins an opera, *Olav Trygvason,* based on a story by Björnson.

1874   The playwright Ibsen invites Grieg to write incidental music for his drama *Peer Gynt.*

1876   Feb. 28: The first performance of *Peer Gynt* takes place in Christiania, to wide acclaim. Grieg is thirty-two years old.

1877   The Griegs spend the summer in the Hardanger district, where Edvard writes music to the ballad *The Mountain Thrall.*

1878   Grieg's performance of his String Quartet, Violin Sonata, and Piano Concerto in Leipzig are well received.

1879   Edvard Grieg is made conductor of the Bergen Harmonic Society (for two years).

1885   April: The Griegs move into the house specially built for them – Troldhaugen.

1887   Edvard writes a Sonata for Violin and Piano No. 3. The Griegs meet the young English musician Frederick Delius.

1888-89 Grieg makes very successful concert performances in London and Paris.

1892	June 11: Edvard and Nina celebrate their silver wedding anniversary at Troldhaugen.
1894	Grieg writes three volumes of songs based on the settings of Norwegian texts. In Paris, Grieg meets the young French composer, Maurice Ravel.
1895	Mar. : Grieg, aged fifty-one, is seriously unwell with pneumonia.
1897	Dec. : On a visit to England, Grieg performs in front of Queen Victoria.
1898	Due to Grieg's involvement, the first Norwegian Music Festival in Bergen is a great success.
1899	Grieg plays incidental music to *Sigurd Jorsalfar,* at the opening of the National Theater in Christiania. In respose to the Dreyfus Case, Edvard Grieg refuses an invitation to conduct a series of concerts in Paris.
1903	April: Edvard Grieg performs a series of successful concerts in Paris. June: Grieg celebrates his sixtieth birthday. Grieg's transcriptions of Hardanger fiddle tunes, or *Slatter,* are published.
1904	Edvard Grieg meets the German Kaiser, Wilhelm II.
1905	Norway gains political independence from Sweden.
1906	During his last visit to London, Grieg meets the Australian composer, Percy Grainger. Grieg finishes *Four Psalms.* Edvard Grieg's health begins to fail.
1907	Sept. 4: Edvard Grieg dies, aged sixty-four, in Bergen Hospital.

Recommended Listening

"Morning" from *Peer Gynt* – This was written to depict the sunrise in North Africa that the hero Peer Gynt visited in the famous Ibsen play. It has a haunting melody played firstly by the flute, and then the oboe. Near the end, bird song is heard played by the woodwind section.

"In the Hall of the Mountain King" – This music is also from the *Peer Gynt* play. Here Peer is exploring the dark caves deep in the mountain. The music begins very quietly, with a mysterious tune on the bassoon. This tune is repeated eighteen times, each time getting louder, while Peer is attacked by vicious trolls, and finally thrown to the Mountain King.

"Wedding Day at Troldhaugen" – This was firstly a solo piano piece which Grieg composed for his wife to celebrate their twenty-fifth wedding anniversary. He later orchestrated the piece. It is a very happy, joyful melody featuring different percussion instruments – triangle, cymbals, and glockenspiel.

Norwegian Dance No. 2 – This charming piece opens with an oboe tune accompanied by pizzicato (plucked) string instruments. The melody is Grieg's own, but he uses traditional folk dance rhythms to make his music sound Norwegian.

Piano Concerto – This is probably the most famous of all Grieg's works. A timpani roll introduces the first piano entry – a series of descending piano chords, which is then followed by a memorable melody accompanied by a full orchestra. Again, Grieg makes use of Norwegian folk themes.

Four Danish Songs – These are settings of words by Hans Christian Andersen – the famous writer of fairy stories. Grieg displays his gift for melodic invention, and the piano parts also are very unusual.

Glossary

Ballad: A poem or song that tells a story, with a repeating *melody*.

Bass or **Basso:** The lowest male singing voice or part in *harmony*.

Concerto: A piece of music for a solo instrument, accompanied by a full orchestra. It usually has three parts, or movements – fast, slow, fast.

Conservatory/ Conservatoire: A school for teaching music or art.

Dotted rhythm: This is a rhythm in which the first of a pair of notes is followed by a dot, making it longer than the second note. This gives the music an uneven, jerky sound, and is often used in dance music.

Folklore: Unwritten stories, customs, and legends handed down from generation to generation and attached to a particular group of people.

Folk music: The music associated with *folklore.*

Fjord: A long, narrow strip of sea between steep cliffs, which is particularly common in Norway.

Gala concert: A concert held in celebration of a specific occasion.

Goat-horn: As it sounds, this is a hollowed-out horn of a goat, which is then blown down through a mouthpiece.

Harmony: When a combination of musical notes is played simultaneously, forming a chord. The term has come to signify the production of a pleasing sound or tune.

Incidental Music: Music composed to accompany a play.

Interlude: A piece of music which takes place in the interval of another musical or dramatic performance.

Libretto: The words in an *opera* that are set to music.

Lyric: Music that has song like qualities, often "light" rather than "heavy" in emotional content. It can also mean the words of a song.

Melodrama: A play that is very emotional and overdramatic in style.

Melody: A succession of musical notes that make up a piece of music.

Norse: Relating to Norway and its people.

Opera: A dramatic work in which all or most of the performers sing their parts. Opera, as it is known today, was first performed in Italy in the early 1600s.

Oratorio: A musical, dramatic composition, usually on a religious theme.

Orchestral Suite: A piece of instrumental music in several movements.

Philharmonic: An orchestra, or group of musicians who are devoted to music.

Pianissimo: To play a musical phrase or piece very softly.

Romantic tradition: The musical style that was popular between about 1810 and 1900. The music was often emotional and dramatic, using freer forms than those used by classical composers. The orchestra was larger, and new instruments were developed. Composers were very interested in the other arts, and often their music was based around stories, poems or pictures.

Score: A composition in which the music for the instruments is written down formally on a page.

Sonata: A musical composition, usually for piano, or solo instrument with piano accompaniment. It is often in three or more movements, or parts.

Soprano: The highest female or male boy's singing voice.

String quartet: A piece music written for string players – two violins, viola and cello. The group of instruments is also called a string quartet.

Symphony: A long composition for orchestra. It is usually in the form of a sonata and made up of three or four movements.

Virtuoso: A recognized master of a particular field, such as music.

Zither: A stringed instrument, originating from the folk music of Austria.

Index

Anitra's Dance 58

Bach, Johann Sebastian 12
Bergen 7-9
  Festival 53-54
  Harmonic Society 39
Berlioz, Hector 25
Beyer, Frants and Marie 40-41
Bjørnson, Bjørnsterne 26, 30-31, 46, 55

Copenhagen 15-16, 28

Dale, Knut 50
Debussy, Claude 25, 47, 56
Delius, Frederick 42-44, 46
Dreyfus case, The 54-55

Edwards, Bella 52
Elegiac Melodies 45

Feddersen, Benjamin 22
Four Danish Songs, see Four "Romances"
Four Piano Pieces 14
Four Psalms 59
Four "Romances" 18
Four Songs for Alto 14
Funeral March for Rikard Nordraak 23, 60

Gade, Niels 16
Grainger, Percy 58-60
Grieg, Alexandra 27-28
Grieg, Edvard
  awards 30, 49, 52, 59
  birth 8
  birth and death of daughter 27, 28
  childhood 8
  as composer 5, 6, 9
  concert tours by 45, 51, 56, 59
  as conductor 24-25, 39, 45, 52, 55
  criticism of 47
  death of 60
  family of 6-8
  friendship with Frederick Delius 42-44
  ill health 14, 48, 52
  influence of folk music and poetry on 20-23, 26, 27, 28-29, 38-39
  marriage to Nina Hagerup 26
  musical compositions
    Anitra's Dance 58
    cello sonata 40
    Elegiac Melodies 45
    Four Danish Songs, see Four "Romances"
    Four Piano Pieces 14
    Four Psalms 59
    Four "Romances" 18, 62
    Four Songs for Alto 14
    Funeral March for Rikard Nordraak 23, 60

Holberg Suite 45
Humoreskes 61
"The Last Spring" 45
Lyric Pieces 26, 40, 47, 49
Melodies of the Heart 18
Mountain Thrall, The 38
Nineteen Norwegian Folk Tunes 50
Old Norwegian Melody with Variations 50
Peer Gynt 6, 31-36, 46-47, 56, 62
  Halling 35
  "In the Hall of the Mountain King" 34, 62
  Springdans 35
Piano Concerto in A minor 6, 14, 22, 27-28, 30, 39, 45-46, 51, 52, 56, 59, 60, 62
piano sonata 24
Slåtter 50
songs of 18, 29, 37, 39, 41, 49
String Quartet in G minor 38-39
Symphony in C minor 16
Symphonic Dances 50
Twenty-five Norwegian Dances and Songs 20
violin sonatas 24, 39, 42-45
Violin Sonata in F major 39
Violin Sonata in G major 44
"Wedding Day at Troldhaugen" 47, 49, 62
partnership with Bjørnson 30, 46-47
partnership with Ibsen 32, 34-37
as pianist 8, 14
relationship with Elise Schjelderup 40
schooldays 9-10
sixtieth birthday 56
studies at Leipzig Conservatory 12-14
Grieg, Nina (née Hagerup) 17-18, 26-27, 37-38, 40-41, 44, 48-49 52

Hagerup, Nina see Grieg, Nina
Halvorsen, Johan 43-44
Hardanger fiddle 10, 19-20, 35, 50
Holberg Suite 45
Horneman, Emil 22

Ibsen, Henrik 6, 30, 32, 34, 36-37, 41

Landsmål 39, 49
Langeleik 20
"The Last Spring" 45
Leipzig Conservatory 11-15, 43
Leipzig Gewandhaus Orchestra 13

Liszt, Franz 28-30
Lyric Pieces 26, 40, 47, 49

Melodies of the Heart 18
Mendelssohn, Felix 12, 25
Moscheles, Ignaz 13
Mountain Melodies Old and New 28
Mountain Thrall, The 38

National Theater, The 11, 15, 31, 32, 54, 56
Nineteen Norwegian Folk Tunes 50
Nordraak, Rikard 18, 22-24
  Funeral March for 23, 60
Norway
  cultural heritage of 8, 30, 32, 37
  dialect of 39
  folk dances of 20, 30
  folk music of 19-20
  history of 10, 11, 58

Olav Trygvason 30-31
Old Norwegian Melody with Variations 50
Ole Bull 10-11, 19, 29, 31-32, 39

Peer Gynt 6, 31-36, 46-47, 56, 62
  Halling 35
  "In the Hall of the Mountain King" 34, 62
  Springdans 35
Piano Concerto in A minor 6, 14, 22, 27-28, 30, 39, 45-46, 51-52 56, 59-60, 62
Plaidy, Louis 13

Ravel, Maurice 51
Röntgen, Julius 46-47, 49

Schjelderup, Elise 40
Schumann, Clara 13-14
Schumann, Robert 13-14, 56
Sigurd Jorsalfar 30, 55
Sinding, Christian 43-44, 46
Slåtter 20, 50
Snow Queen, The 18
Songs 18, 29, 37, 39, 41, 49
String Quartet in G minor 38-39
Symphonic Dances 50
Symphony in C minor 16

Trolls 33, 35, 41
Tua, Teresina 42
Twenty-five Norwegian Dances and Songs 20

Violin sonatas 24, 42-43, 45
Violin Sonata in F major 39
Violin Sonata in G major 44

Wagner, Richard 25, 40, 56
"Wedding Day at Troldhaugen" 47, 49, 62
Wenzel, Ernst Ferdinand 13